ALLEN PHOTOGI

CW00969986

WALKING A
CROSS-COUNTRY COURSE

CONTENTS

ROUTINE WALKING

For nearly all event riders, it is the thrill of riding across country that is the motivation behind competing in horse trials.

Walking the cross-country course is an essential part of the competition, allowing riders to familiarise themselves with the jumps, whilst also working out the best way to tackle the course. The course walk enables riders to look at how the ground conditions and terrain change on the approach to each fence and how they will have to alter the speed and direction of their approach accordingly. A good way to check that you are taking the shortest, most direct route between fences in order to save time is to look behind you to the previous fence when walking the course – this will show you that the line you have walked may not be the quickest.

At a major three-day event, most riders will walk the course at least three times. The first walk is to get a general impression and view of the course. During the second walk, riders examine alternative routes and during the final walk they will decide exactly which routes to take. At a one-day event, riders will probably walk the course once – only because that is all time permits! At a three-day event it is a good idea to walk the course at different times of the day so that you will have an idea as to how the light (sunshine or otherwise) will affect each fence.

It is also advisable to beg, steal or borrow a wheel to measure the course. Check the speed required for your course (i.e. metres per minute). Then, measure off each minute marker on the course,

this helps you to ride to time. By checking your stopwatch at each marker you can see whether there is any need to adjust your speed. (You need to practise checking/ glancing at your watch whilst riding at home.)

During your walk, check where the marker flags direct you to go and where the red and white flags are on the jumps. Tackling the jump on the wrong side of the flags leads to instant elimination – sometimes easily done!

THE START

The first couple of fences on most cross-country courses will be fairly straightforward with the course designer having the aim of starting the horses off well and getting horse and rider focused on the task in hand.

At the beginning it is vital that you get your horse into a good and relaxed rhythm with as little interference as possible from the rider. By the time that you arrive at the third or fourth fence, it is more than likely the designer will begin to ask more of you

and by this stage it is important for the horse and rider to be paying attention and to be prepared.

AUTHOR'S TIP

It is important for the rider to remember that the horse never gets the opportunity to see the fences and course until he is galloping round it. Riders must be aware of the ground conditions throughout.

Mental Attitude

During the course walk, examine every possible route, be confident that both you and your horse will get to the other side of every fence and make it through the finish. I am well known for being highly superstitious and always walk through the start and finish in the hope that I will then at least complete the course!

By the end of the walk you should be confident that you will get round successfully. Be realistic about the various options the course designer has presented. Ideally, I would always choose to go the quick route but, depending on the horse's experience and the weather conditions, I would always have an open mind.

Bearing in mind your horse's capabilities and experience, by the end of your walk you should be clear on which routes you will take. Setting off with any doubts in your mind can only lead to trouble. Never change plans en route unless you have full knowledge of the alternative and I feel that any late changes should only be to take an easier option.

Before you know it you will be galloping through the finish, hopefully with a successful round under your belt. It is important to keep your concentration right up to the last fence.

Never forget about your horse's welfare at the end of your round. What you must not do at the end of the cross-country is think, 'Great, I've finished!', let go of your reins, gallop through the finish and let the horse end in a heap. It is at the end of your round that the horse's legs are most vulnerable. Slow down and come back to walk, in balance and not too abruptly.

AUTHOR'S TIP

Remember you haven't won until you've gone through the finish flags. Don't blow it at the last fence by taking liberties.

PACE AND SPEED

Always think about the pace and speed you wish to achieve during your round. Rhythm is one of the most important factors and probably the key element to completing your round successfully and safely within the time.

After the landing at each fence, get back into your rhythm as soon as possible. Do not waste time patting your horse or your-self until you are back into full swing. This is when the time you have taken to walk the course properly will be invaluable.

The more horses you ride and the more you compete, the easier it is to develop the correct feel for the speed at which you should be riding. Many of the top riders are very clever in the way they use the terrain and the approach to fences, maintaining the correct rhythm and saving valuable seconds (again, good course walking).

Balanced but wasting no time, Arakai and I exit from the lake at Badminton.

AUTHOR'S TIP

Be able to use your whip in both hands and practise changing hands whilst galloping. This will help keep your horse straight and accurate, especially at angled fences and corners.

APPROACHES AND LANDINGS

When walking the course, make sure you walk the exact line you intend to jump. The right approach is essential for accuracy, safety and to save time. Be positive, think ahead, look up and keep your leg on when approaching cross-country fences. Remember you have seen the course before, your horse has not!

The more technical the fence is, the more accurate your lines have to be. For example, angled rails or corners ride better if lines are accurate but also if the horse is in balance. The same applies to downhill fences. These should be approached slowly, with plenty of impulsion and with the horse sitting on his quarters so that he is not on his forehand at point of take-off (i.e. his hocks are engaged).

In these photographs Arakai and I demonstrate the importance of balance and working as a partnership. I am looking towards the next fence in anticipation of the turn.

COMMON FENCES

During a cross-country round, riders come across a wide variety of fences and by walking the course correctly you should have a clear insight into how to tackle each one. At the start of the round, the aim is to settle the horse into a good rhythm and give him confidence over the first few fences. Once this has been established, you can then start to increase speed.

Whenever possible, always approach your fences straight and in the middle. Later, experience will allow for angled fences and cutting corners.

The photograph above shows Stanwick Ghost going very straight; although my elbows are out I am maintaining contact.

LOGS

A good solid log fence is the ideal jump to get you away in the early stages of your round. Most horses respect such fences and will give you a good clean jump. This will help to give you the confidence as you gallop on your way.

UPRIGHTS

Care should be taken on the approach to very upright fences. If an upright gate or set of rails comes well into the course, your horse may be getting a little 'long' and it is important to re-balance and possibly take the time and care to 'showjump' the fence before moving on.

Leslie Law is seen jumping an upright with ease.

SPREADS

On any cross-country course there will be a number of spread fences. When walking the course look out for any obstacles which will get in the way of your approach to a spread fence as you will need more impulsion and possible increase of pace for the width of the fence. Here A Mouse Called Mickey shows his enormous scope.

It is important not to break your rhythm round the course and the speed should be directly related to the type of problems presented by the course designer. Big, bold, inviting fences can be tackled with a little more pace than more technical, upright combinations. When jumping fences that require the horse to be bold and lengthen his stride it is important he does not back off. Keep the horse on the aids. He should be 'in front of your leg' (i.e. responsive to your legs).

If a horse dwells in the air over a fence this is often because he lacks confidence or experience. If this happens ride away from

the fence a little more strongly and with more determination. If the problem continues to happen then more schooling at home might be necessary, or a lower standard of competition would be more suitable, to restore confidence.

In the photo above Arakai is seen in full stretch over the drays at Belton.

ARROWHEADS

Jumping arrowheads is a test of keeping your horse straight and maintaining accuracy. Much of your success at an event is down to training at home and this type of fence can be practised by using barrels and poles to accustom your horse to jumping narrow obstacles.

When approaching arrowheads, maintain the correct line to the spot on the fence you have chosen to jump, look forward and keep hold, riding on the contact but not too fast. Prepare the horse on the approach, keep the canter round and connected and most of all maintain your straightness.

Here the rider has a choice between taking the narrow tree stump at the bottom of the hill or of swinging left-handed to jump the longer, easier alternative.

AUTHOR'S TIP

Remember, the faster you ride arrowheads the more difficult it is to be accurate.

COMBINATIONS

When walking the course, make sure you measure the distances correctly and know your horse's length of stride. Choose your line through a combination clearly and have points on the fence, or something in the distance to aim at, in order to keep straight.

The horse and rider shown below are in perfect balance.

Combination fences, either on a straight line or on a turn, can be technically difficult. Therefore, a balanced approach is a must and good course walking is essential to know how much pace your horse will need to approach each type of combination you are presented with. Below, Arakai jumps confidently and lands in balance to make the ditch appear easier than it is.

HOLLOWS

Hollows (formerly known as coffins) require careful thought and consideration and should be tackled from a short, powerful stride. By coming in with too much speed the horse can easily be surprised by the fence when he suddenly sees the ditch. If the fence into the complex is very upright and tight for distance, the horse will need to be on a short, bouncy stride with a lot of control.

The hollow or sunken road type of fence is not a combination where riders should expect to save too much time. It is important to be very straight on the approach and remember to keep the horse's 'engine' (i.e. back legs and quarters) engaged.

The Moose shows the effort required. Riding 'backwards' on the last few strides will only cause problems and leave the horse with insufficient energy to tackle the complex.

WATER

Over the years I have, when-ever possible, and especially at the major three-day events, taken the opportunity to walk through the water. This gives you a better understanding of how deep the water is, what the footing is like underneath and what the horse faces if there is a jump out of the water or an island out of one section and into another. When trotting or cantering through the water, maintain your line to the jump out and keep a good, strong rhythm. Here Stanwick Ghost jumps confidently into the water at Belton Park.

If the water is deep it can have a very dragging effect on the horse making it more difficult to maintain the correct pace, and the spray doesn't help either.

Jumping into water is probably the biggest demand to ask of a horse's courage as he does not know how deep it is going to be. Because of this, a powerful canter is required with a positive approach but, never let it be too long and flat. Some falls happen coming out of water which can be caused by awkward distances between elements or some horses are affected by the splashing of the water and they can easily lose their concentration. However, by maintaining your balance, impulsion and rhythm, and not looking too much for a stride, you should give your horse every opportunity to jump out well (*see* Kilcoran *opposite*). If your horse falls into a trot in the water it is best to continue in a powerful trot and not try to regain canter – horses are less likely to miss their stride from trot.

CORNERS

Like arrowheads, these should be practised at home using showjumps. Walking the correct line at corner fences is a must, they probably cause more trouble than any other type of jump. The proper way is to have an imaginary line dissecting the corner exactly halfway through, then, plan your approach to ride that line at 90 degrees (i.e. straight). It can often be helpful to find some obvious landmark in the distance to line up with (i.e. a tree or some other tall and distinctive feature that you can pick out easily at a canter).

In this technical double of corners the line should be from the red flag of 25 to the white flag of 26.

It is also very important that you maintain contact to the point of take-off – to soften the hands too early gives the horse every opportunity to take avoiding action!

Carry your whip in the hand that is nearest to the point of the corner to help straightness. In this case I would have my whip in my left hand because of the second corner but you have to assess the situation according to your horse.

BANKS

Banks and steps up are fences where the rider needs to get well forward in the saddle. They require a lot of physical effort and therefore should be taken with maximum impulsion. Do not allow the stride to get too long, keep the horse collected in order to create the necessary spring to jump up the bank.

When tackling a number of steps up, it is important that you do not allow the energy level to fade away on the way up. If the steps are jumped downwards, the rider must not allow their weight to fall forward. Ideally the rider's shoulders should be back and he should be looking ahead. When there are two or more steps down, it can be helpful to maintain canter on the approach so that the horse does not hesitate and make the jump uncomfortable for both of you.

Jeanette Brakewell, riding at Badminton, looks secure and balanced.

DROP FENCES

Ruth Williams negotiates a drop a Thirlestane. This type of fence is usually more off-putting to the rider than the horse but the correct approach is vital. If you come at the fence 'long and loose' and the horse stands off, he will suddenly see the drop and put the brakes on in midair. This can cause him to drop his hind legs on the fence and probably peck on landing.

In order to jump a drop fence well, come in in a powerful, bouncy canter. Get the horse as close as you can so that he jumps it in a round way and lands in balance. I am a great believer in the 'safe seat' at drop fences and into water. But, although the upper body leans back, the horse must not be restricted by the reins (you should slip the reins) and your lower leg should remain in position. Ideally, the leg should not swing backwards but neither should it push forward so that you lock the knee and remove all the suppleness from your seat.

Here Jaybee jumps a spread drop fence which needs a bit more pace.

JUMPING FROM LIGHT INTO DARK AND DARK INTO LIGHT

Bear in mind when walking the course how changes in light may affect the way a jump appears to the horse. When this happens, always give the horse a little more time to assess what he has to do.

It is a good idea to walk the course the day before at the same time as you will be riding – for example the light will change throughout the day at the bridge shown in the photo below.

DITCHES AND TRAKEHNERS

Trakehners are fences which usually look much worse to the rider when walking the course than they do to the horse. Riders must remember that the horse does not stand at the fence and look down into the ditch as he is approaching at a strong, powerful canter or gallop.

The horse should be 'in front' of your leg and that way, his head and your head will be up and looking forward, making the jump easy; never look down or drop your horse's head when approaching ditches.

Looking up and forward, Arakai makes nothing of this ditch.

BOUNCES

The bounce fence requires both horse and rider to be athletic and in harmony (see the sequence of photos opposite). A good, controlled approach is important with not too much speed but plenty of impulsion.

Keep the rhythm on the approach and maintain your balance throughout the effort. A bounce into water needs a more positive approach.

Keep with the horse as he jumps, getting left behind will only make the bounce more

difficult to negotiate safely. You must never gallop too fast into bounces but if you lack enough commitment and your horse has to try and stride it then being in balance and ready for anything is all you can do to help your horse!

AUTHOR'S TIP

If any of the cross-country fences are near to the stables or horsebox park, always be aware that horses may 'hang' towards this area. Horses naturally want to head for home so make sure that you are aware of what they could be thinking whilst they are on the course.

SEEING A STRIDE

It is not essential to be able to 'see a stride' but helpful if you can. The main point to remember is that to ride cross-country fences successfully and well it is down to the rider being able to remain balanced while keeping the horse in good balance and rhythm with enough impulsion to jump the fences throughout the course. If the horse is working for you and with you and at a speed he is comfortable with, then the right stride will come without too much searching.

Although the horse seen here (*above*) has taken off close to the fence both horse and rider look comfortable.

TIMING

Timing is obviously very important if you want to win your event. But, before you try to win, ride a few courses at each level without a stopwatch. Try to learn to feel the correct speed. Your time will be better if you can ride in a good rhythm throughout rather than at a mad gallop between fences and then have a fight to get control at each jump.

ONE-DAY EVENTS

At one-day events, time should never be the major consideration and so I never wear a stopwatch, preferring to ride the course according to my horse's level of experience and how he feels on the day. (Remember, they, like us, have good and bad days!)

AUTHOR'S TIP

The start box can be a tense time and it is important to keep calm and focused.

THREE-DAY EVENTS

At a three-day event there is usually an official course walk the day before the competition gets underway. Competitors are driven round the first phase of the roads and tracks, then they walk the steeplechase and are then driven round the remainder of the roads and tracks.

For roads and tracks you should try to average four minutes per kilometre at a sensible trot, that will give you plenty of time, if you have the opportunity to measure the course, to work out your timings and where you should be on the course by a certain time. You will

need to borrow a measuring wheel for this, or walk with someone who has one, or get some kind person to tell you where the minute markers are – provided you trust them!

When you measure the course, it is important to walk the direct route as the designer will have measured the course on the tightest possible line. It is now that you should ride with a stopwatch to help you ride to time. Arakai is seen here (*right*) on the steeplechase at Badminton – note the stopwatch on my left wrist.

The way you set about riding the cross-country course will depend on a number of factors. These include the weather; state of the ground; whether you are going out to win or just to get round for experience, and the length of the course.

But, whatever the circumstances (i.e. horse's experience and stamina), it is essential that you set out on the cross-country in determined mood.

COMPETITORS

Riders will often walk the course together and help each other with ideas on how to ride particularly demanding fences. I think that it is one of the best things about the sport, because it involves both horse and rider working as a partnership to reach the end of the course successfully – as seen here with Rangitoto. It is not just about the rider.

Whether you are just starting your eventing career or moving up the grades, never be afraid to ask advice from the experienced senior riders. We've all been in your shoes and are only too willing to help if we can.

I wish you happy and safe eventing.

ACKNOWLEDGEMENTS

The majority of photographs in this book were supplied by
Tim Smith and he and Ian Stark are grateful to Seven Seas Pet and
Animal Health Care and Expo Life for their help in supplying
additional photographs.

British Library Cataloguing-in-Publication Data.
A catalogue record for this book is available from the British Library

ISBN 0.85131.793.6

Published in Great Britain in 2000 by
J. A. Allen an imprint of Robert Hale Ltd.,
Clerkenwell House, 45–47 Clerkenwell Green,
London EC1R 0HT

Design and Typesetting by Paul Saunders
Edited by John Beaton
Series editor Jane Lake
Colour processing by Tenon & Polert Colour Scanning Ltd., Hong Kong
Printed in Hong Kong by Dah Hua Printing Press Co. Ltd.